# Leonardo da Vinci

## Renaissance Artist and Inventor

Stephanie Kuligowski, M.A.T.

## Publishing Credits

Dona Herweck Rice, *Editor-in-Chief*
Lee Aucoin, *Creative Director*
Torrey Maloof, *Editor*
Neri Garcia, *Senior Designer*
Stephanie Reid, *Photo Researcher*
Rachelle Cracchiolo, M.S.Ed., *Publisher*

## Image Credits

cover (left) North Wind Picture Archives, cover (right) Getty Images; p.1 Northwind Pictures Archives; p.4 Getty Images; p.5 North Wind Picture Archives; p.6 (top) Shutterstock, Inc.; p.6 (bottom) Bridgeman Art Library; p.7 (top) The Granger Collection; p.7 (bottom) Shutterstock, Inc.; p.8 Shutterstock, Inc.; p.8–9 iStockphoto; p.10 (top) Bridgeman Art Library; p.10 (bottom) The Granger Collection; p.11 The Granger Collection; p.12 Getty Images; p.13 The Granger Collection; p.14 (left) The Granger Collection; p.14 (right) Super Stock; p.15 The Granger Collection; p.16 Shutterstock, Inc.; p.16–17 Bridgeman Art Library; p.18 Public Domain; p.19 (left) North Wind Picture Archives; p.19 (right) Teacher Created Materials; p.20 (left) Getty Images; p.20 (right) Getty Images; p.21 (left) Bridgeman Art Library; p.21 (right) Shutterstock, Inc.; p.22 The Granger Collection; p.23 (top) Shutterstock, Inc.; p.23 (bottom left) Bridgeman Art Library; p.23 (bottom right) Newscom; p.24 Bridgeman Art Library; p.25 (top) Getty Images; p.25 (bottom) Bridgeman Art Library; p.26 Public Domain; p.26–27 Shutterstock, Inc.; p.27 Shutterstock, Inc.; p.29 (top) Getty Images; p.29 (bottom) Getty Images; p.32 Bridgeman Art Library; back cover Shutterstock, Inc.

---

**Teacher Created Materials**
5301 Oceanus Drive
Huntington Beach, CA 92649-1030
http://www.tcmpub.com

**ISBN 978-1-4333-5008-5**

# Table of Contents

# Renaissance Man

For nearly a thousand years, the people of Europe struggled to survive from day to day. They worked to put food on the table and to fend off attacks from conquerors. Also, the Roman Catholic Church taught them to focus on heaven rather than earth. Many people stopped examining the world and creating art.

In the late 1300s, change came to Italy. Europeans had begun to trade with Asia, and Italy was located along the main trade route. As more goods came from Asia, more wealth flowed into Italian hands.

merchants in Venice

an artist painting in Florence during the Renaissance

The new wealth meant that people had more free time and spending money. They read, studied, painted, sculpted, and played music. They questioned old ideas and made new discoveries. Western culture experienced a rebirth. The French call a rebirth a ***renaissance*** (reh-nuh-SAWNTS). This time period is known as the Renaissance.

No one embodied the spirit of the Renaissance better than Leonardo da Vinci (lee-uh-NAHR-doh duh VIN-chee). He was trained as a painter. But, he also worked as a musician, a scientist, an **engineer**, and an inventor. His boundless curiosity guided his life.

## Ancient History

At the beginning of the Renaissance, scholars in Italy rediscovered the texts, buildings, sculptures, and ideas of ancient Rome. For about a thousand years, these great works had been ignored. Suddenly, people were inspired to build on the legacy of that great society.

## At the Epicenter

The changes that marked the Renaissance came first to Florence, Italy. **Merchants** there organized themselves into **guilds**, or groups of skilled workers. Each guild made rules for its workers and got involved in local politics. Under this system, Florence thrived. Leonardo da Vinci moved to this exciting city when he was 15 years old.

# The Young da Vinci

## Humble Birth

Leonardo da Vinci was born on April 15, 1452. His family lived in the small village of Vinci near Florence, Italy. His father's family had lived in the village for hundreds of years. They had even taken the village's name as their last name.

Da Vinci's father, Ser Piero (sair pee-AIR-oh) da Vinci, was a respected lawyer. His mother, Caterina, came from a poor family. Da Vinci's parents were not married. They could never marry because they came from different social classes.

Vinci, Italy

da Vinci writing down his ideas

fifteenth-century Florence, Italy

At that time, a child born outside of marriage was thought to be an embarrassment. Such children were called ***illegitimate***. They had limited options in life. They could not go to college or hold certain jobs. As the child of unmarried parents, da Vinci's future was uncertain from the start.

Just months after da Vinci was born, Ser Piero married a girl from a wealthy family. The couple moved to Florence, about 30 miles (48 km) from Vinci. Da Vinci lived with his mother for the first year of his life. Then, Caterina married and moved to a nearby town. Young da Vinci stayed in Vinci with his father's parents, Antonio and Lucia da Vinci.

## Family Matters

During his early years, da Vinci spent most of his time with his grandparents. Da Vinci's mother went on to have five other children. She probably saw her oldest son just a few times a year. Da Vinci's father most likely spent even less time with his son.

## Feathered Friend

Da Vinci said his first memory came from infancy. He remembered a bird flying over his craddle. It swooped down and touched his face. Da Vinci wondered if this event launched his lifelong interest in flight.

This is the bird da Vinci remembered seeing as a child, a European black kite.

## Country Boy

Leonardo da Vinci was not born into an easy situation. His mom and dad were not married. Their family backgrounds kept them from marrying each other. Still, the da Vinci family lived a comfortable life.

For generations, the men of the family had worked as **notaries**. Notaries witnessed the making of documents. The da Vincis owned land that had olive groves, vineyards, and wheat fields. They lived in a large home and had books to read and instruments to play.

As a boy, da Vinci studied reading, writing, and math. Boys from wealthy families went to school to learn Latin. But, da Vinci was taught at home, probably by his grandmother.

an Italian vineyard today

He did not learn Latin because he would never be allowed to enter a profession that used Latin. Da Vinci did learn to play the **lyre** (LAHY-er), a stringed instrument. He was a talented musician with a beautiful voice.

Da Vinci was also lucky to have his young uncle, Francesco (fran-CHES-koh), as a friend. Francesco farmed the family's land. Da Vinci often followed him into the fields. It was there that da Vinci learned about nature. He was interested in water and animals, especially birds. His curiosity about the natural world would last his whole life.

## Future Farmer

Da Vinci could not be a notary like his father. Notaries had to be sons of married parents. Da Vinci's grandparents might have encouraged him to follow in his Uncle Francesco's footsteps. Farming would have been a suitable trade for a young man in da Vinci's position.

## Lefty for Life

Da Vinci was left handed. At that time, people believed that being left handed was the work of the devil. Most parents and teachers forced left-handed children to use their right hands instead. But da Vinci continued to write, draw, and paint with his left hand throughout his life. This helped him later in life when the right side of his body became paralyzed, or unable to move. Because he was able to use his left hand, he could still paint and draw.

## Star Student

When da Vinci was in his early teens, several events changed his life. His grandparents, with whom he had spent most of his life, died. His Uncle Francesco got married. And his father, Ser Piero, moved to Florece where the Medici (MED-i-chee) family lived. The Medicis were the most powerful family in Florence. They were connected to the important people in the city.

Andrea del Verrocchio

Da Vinci moved to Florence to live with his father. Ser Piero got his son a position as an **apprentice** to an artist. An apprentice works with a professional in order to learn a **trade**, or skill. The professional artist, Andrea del Verrocchio (AHN-drey-uh del vuh-ROH-kee-oh), was the best in Florence. He ran a workshop that operated like a factory. Many apprentices worked together to produce works of art. They made **altarpieces** for churches, portraits for wealthy residents, costumes for plays, suits of armor, and even tombstones.

a Renaissance painter and his apprentice

The apprentices helped Verrocchio complete each piece. They made paintbrushes, mixed paints, copied his sketches onto canvases, and cleaned the shop. In this way, they learned a trade that would provide them with a good living. Da Vinci's natural talent was evident from the start. He was Verrocchio's best apprentice.

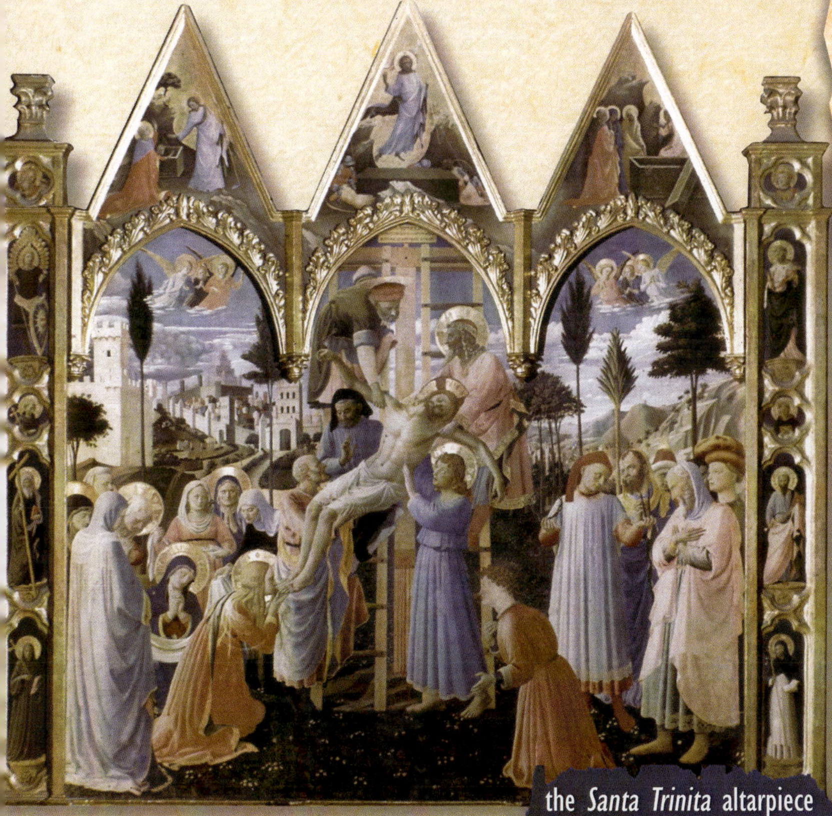

the *Santa Trinita* altarpiece in Florence, Italy

## Learning from a Master

Andrea del Verrocchio was born in Florence in 1435. He was trained as a goldsmith but was also a skilled painter and sculptor. Verrocchio trained many artists who became Renaissance masters, including Sandro Botticelli (SAHN-droh bot-i-CHEL-ee).

## Canvases, Brushes, and...Chickens?

An artist's workshop, like Verrocchio's, would have been stocked with many things, including chickens. Artists kept chickens for their eggs. Egg yolks, powdered colors, and water were mixed to make tempera (TEM-per-uh) paint. The powdered colors were ground-up minerals, plants, lead, and even a semiprecious stone called *lapis lazuli* (LAP-is LAZ-oo-lee).

# Time to Work

## On His Own

A painter's apprentice usually trained with a master artist for six years. After that, an apprentice could join the local painters' guild. In Italy, guilds had been organized for almost every trade. These guilds made rules for the trades, helped their members, and were involved in local politics. To open a workshop, a painter had to be a member of the painters' guild.

Da Vinci finished his training with Verrocchio in 1472 at the age of 20. He joined the painters' guild in Florence that same year. Still, da Vinci kept working for Verrocchio as an assistant. During this time, he completed one of his first solo paintings, *The Annunciation.*

da Vinci's painting, *The Annunciation*

members of the Medici family

After six years as Verrocchio's assistant, da Vinci opened his own workshop. In 1478, he was hired to paint an altarpiece for the Chapel of Saint Bernard in Florence. He took on an apprentice and started the painting, but he never completed it.

This was to become a trend for da Vinci. Throughout his career, he left many projects unfinished.

### The Arts Thrive

Florence was a center of trade during the Renaissance. The city's merchants and church leaders were getting rich. They wanted to show off their new wealth. To do this, they became **patrons** of the arts. They hired artists to paint portraits of them and their loved ones. They paid artists to decorate churches and public spaces. The Catholic Church and the Medici family were two of the biggest art patrons in Italy.

### Curiosity

Da Vinci had a hard time finishing projects. One reason may have been his curiosity about the world around him. He was curious about everything! His busy mind might have made it hard to focus on one project for long. Da Vinci constantly wanted to learn and study new things.

## Working for the Duke

At the age of 30, da Vinci was not the successful artist he had hoped to become. He had very few customers. Of the two major projects he had been hired to paint, he failed to complete either. Perhaps da Vinci was ready for a fresh start. In 1482, he moved to Milan (mih-LAHN).

Some scholars say that da Vinci got a job as a court musician for Ludovico Sforza (loo-doh-VEE-koh SFAWRT-suh), the Duke of Milan. Others say that the duke hired da Vinci as an engineer and painter. In a letter to the duke, da Vinci listed the ways he could be of service. First on the list was working as an engineer. Da Vinci said he could design bridges and build weapons. Painter was last on the list.

da Vinci's sketches of weapons

In Milan, da Vinci made himself at home in the duke's court. He set up a workshop to paint, design buildings, and make theater costumes and sets. The duke threw elaborate parties for which da Vinci designed decorations. Sometimes, he even acted as master of ceremonies at the events. Da Vinci lived an exciting life in Milan for 17 years.

### Life of Luxury

By the 1480s, da Vinci's talent was well known across Italy. Having the young artist in his court made the duke look good. The duke paid da Vinci well most of the time. But, when the cost of war drained the family fortune, the duke got creative with his payments. Once, he gave da Vinci a vineyard!

### A Big Job

In 1489, the duke asked da Vinci to build a huge bronze statue of the duke's father on horseback. Before da Vinci cast it, the French attacked Milan. The bronze was needed for cannons instead of statues.

## Failed Experiment

*The Last Supper* was to be a **fresco**. This was a technique in which an artist plastered a wall and then painted the wet plaster with watercolors. The artist had to work quickly before the plaster dried, but the painting would last for centuries.

Da Vinci was a slow worker, so he tried a new method. He let the plaster dry and then painted it with oil and varnish. The experiment seemed to work, but within five years the paint began chipping. *The Last Supper* mural on the church wall has been repaired many times.

## Painting a Masterpiece

Da Vinci's other interests distracted him from painting. During his 17 years in Milan, he completed only six art projects. One of these is considered da Vinci's best work of art, his **masterpiece**. It is said to be one of the greatest paintings of all time.

This is the church where da Vinci's *The Last Supper* is painted on the dining room wall.

The Last Supper

In 1495, the Duke of Milan had da Vinci paint a dining room wall in a church. The chosen scene was from the Bible. It would show Jesus eating with his followers on the night before he died. In the Christian religion, this event is called "the Last Supper."

For years, da Vinci worked on this painting. He started with sketches in his notebooks. He worked hard to get the **perspective** just right. Perspective is a technique for making some objects seem farther away than others.

Da Vinci also invented a new painting technique for the mural. He covered the wall with plaster and then painted it with a mixture of oil and varnish. He hoped this would allow him to work at his own pace.

The finished mural was a marvel. Each figure had a unique posture and expression. *The Last Supper* was one of da Vinci's greatest masterpieces.

# Other Interests

## Taking Note

Da Vinci was trained as a painter, but art was not his only interest. As a young man, da Vinci began writing his many ideas in notebooks. He sketched figures and drew plans for machines. He wrote letters. He took notes about subjects that fascinated him. Some scholars think da Vinci wrote 20,000 pages during his life. About 6,000 of those pages have been found. They provide insight into the mind of a genius.

Da Vinci's notes show a new way to look at the world. In the past, the daily struggle to survive left little time for curiosity. The Catholic Church also told people to focus on heaven rather than earth. Science had no place in the Middle Ages.

pages from one of da Vinci's notebooks

da Vinci's sketch for raising water

In the 1400s, life began to change. People suddenly had free time and spending money. They began to create art, music, and literature. People began to wonder how the world worked. In his notebooks, da Vinci asked questions, made observations, and drew conclusions. This is similar to the way modern-day scientists conduct research. It is known as **scientific inquiry**.

## Writing Backward

Da Vinci often wrote his ideas backward in his notebooks. This right-to-left writing is called *mirror writing* because it can be read in a mirror. This might have prevented the left-handed da Vinci from smearing the ink.

## Favorite Subjects

More than any other subject, da Vinci wrote about water. He studied and sketched it in all its forms. He designed machines to harness its power. His notebooks also included many sketches of the human body, birds, and different machines he had invented.

## The Great Mystery

At the beginning of his career, **realism** was da Vinci's goal. *Realism* means to paint the world exactly as it is. But during his time in Milan, da Vinci began to want more. He wanted to understand the *hows* and *whys* of life.

Da Vinci was very curious about the human body. He wanted to see bones and muscles. He wanted to know how people moved and how blood traveled through the body. Most of all, he wanted to solve what he called the "great mystery." He wanted to find the soul.

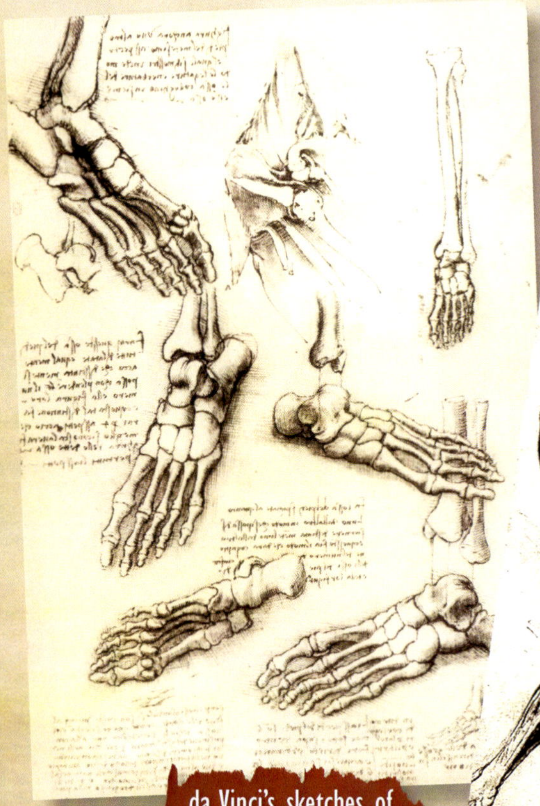

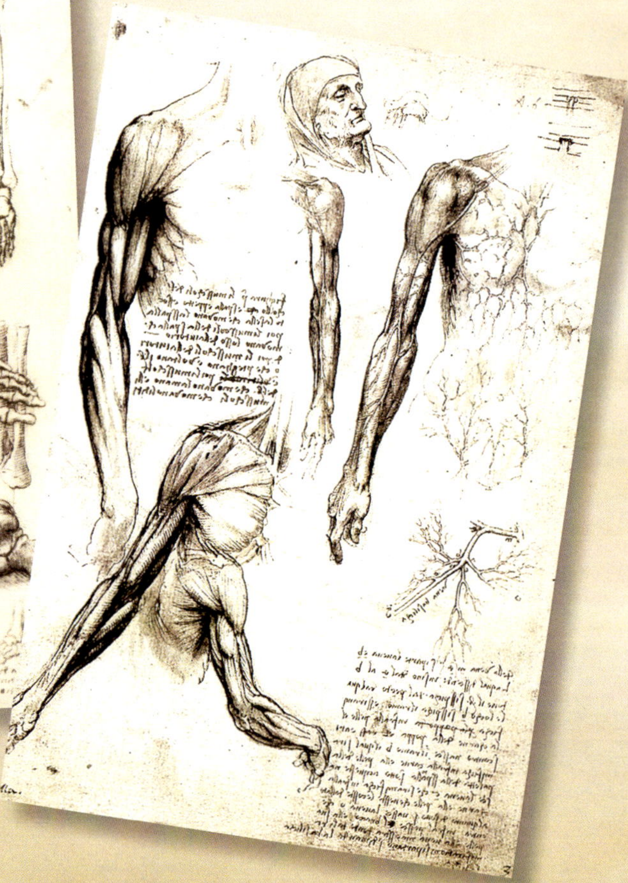

da Vinci's sketches of the human body

*The Virgin and Child with St. Anne* shows da Vinci's knowledge of the human shape.

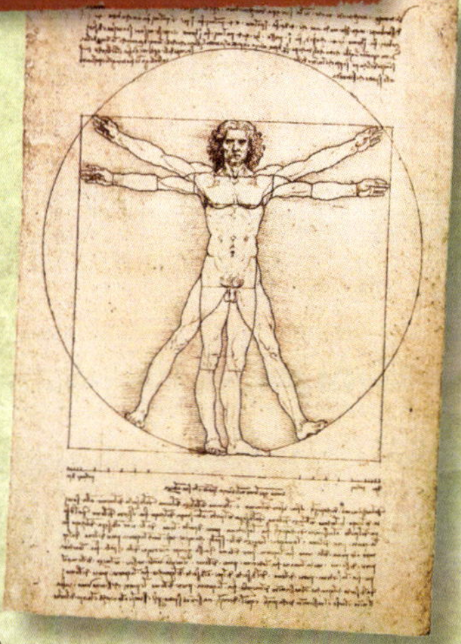

da Vinci's *Vitruvian Man*

To answer these questions, da Vinci **dissected**, or cut apart, dead bodies. He visited the local morgue, the place where the dead bodies were kept until they were buried. Da Vinci would choose a corpse, or dead body, wash it, and cut it open. He spent hours sketching what he saw. Later, he studied his sketches and tried to explain what he had seen. He studied more than 30 bodies. He made 200 detailed drawings of the human body.

### Science and Art

Da Vinci did not study the body to improve his paintings, as many artists did. He wanted to discover the mysteries of human life. But, as a result of his studies, da Vinci's paintings are incredibly lifelike.

### Dirty Work

Cutting apart dead bodies was not a pleasant task. Da Vinci took the risk of catching diseases from the bodies. Often, the bodies began to decay before he had even finished his sketches.

## Inventive Ideas

Da Vinci was a painter, a sculptor, a musician, and a scientist. His notebooks show that he was also an inventor. His studies of the world around him inspired him to invent new machines.

One of da Vinci's favorite subjects was water. He studied and sketched water in all its forms. He listed 64 different words for the way water moves. He designed many devices to use the power of water. Da Vinci designed a canal to link the city of Florence with the ocean. He also sketched designs for life preservers, flippers, paddle-wheel boats, and submarines.

Flight also fascinated da Vinci. He studied and sketched birds to find out how their wings worked. Then, he used what he learned to design flying machines for people. One of da Vinci's machines had wings that spun around in circles. His "airscrew" used the same science that makes modern-day helicopters fly.

Da Vinci's ideas might have seemed far-fetched at the time, but many of his designs have been tested and found to work. He was a thinker ahead of his time.

a paddle-wheel boat constructed from da Vinci's sketches

da Vinci's sketch of an airscrew

## It Really Works!

In his notebook, da Vinci sketched a pyramid-shaped device. He called it a "linen tent" and said it would allow a person to jump from any height safely. Today, we call such a device a *parachute*. In the year 2000, a skydiver wearing a linen tent based on da Vinci's drawings jumped from an airplane. He landed safely and proved that the linen tent worked!

## $30.8 Million!

People today still find da Vinci's notes and ideas to be incredibly valuable. Modern-day inventor and Microsoft founder Bill Gates paid $30.8 million in 1994 to buy one of da Vinci's notebooks.

an airscrew model

Bill Gates

## Military Might

At the turn of the century, Italy was divided into **city-states**. City-states were like small countries. During the Renaissance, the city-states were fighting off attacks by outsiders. The city-states also fought each other. These events inspired da Vinci to find new ways to defend cities and win battles.

In the early 1500s, da Vinci got a new job. He became a military engineer for Cesare Borgia (CHEY-zah-rey BAWR-juh). Borgia was the leader of the pope's armies in Rome. In service to Borgia, da Vinci traveled around Italy for many months. He visited rulers who were loyal to Borgia. His job was to give them ideas on how to defend their cities.

Cesare Borgia

Da Vinci also sketched many designs for weapons. One of the weapons was a type of machine gun. It had 33 barrels that fired 11 cannons at a time. Another design was a giant **crossbow**. It could shoot arrows long distances.

Da Vinci also designed the first tank, or armored car. Many cannons were hooked to a round platform on wheels. The platform was covered by a wooden shell. Eight men rode inside the shell and turned the wheels with cranks. The tank could move in any direction.

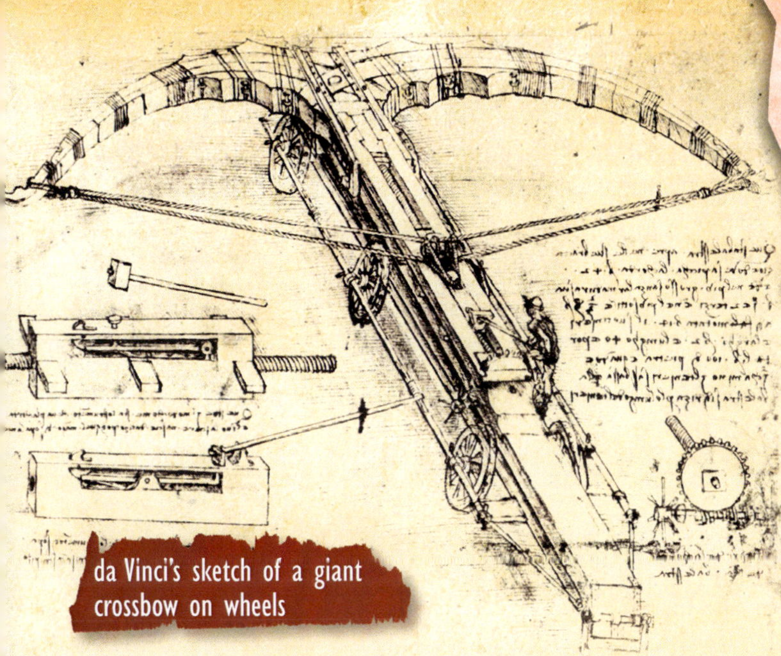

da Vinci's sketch of a giant crossbow on wheels

a model of da Vinci's tank

## A Good Target

Italy was located along important trade routes during the Renaissance. This made many of its city-states rich. Italy became the target of conquerors. It seemed as if everyone wanted a piece of Italy's success. This led to a period of unrest that lasted from 1494 to 1559.

## Powerful Family

Cesare Borgia was the son of Pope Alexander VI, head of the Roman Catholic Church. Like da Vinci, Borgia was born outside of marriage. Nonetheless, Borgia's powerful father gave his son command of the papal armies. The power-hungry Borgia plotted to take over all of Italy.

# A Famous Face

For centuries, one woman's smile has captivated the world. The woman is Mona Lisa. Da Vinci made her famous when he painted her portrait in 1503. Mona Lisa's real name is believed to be Lisa Gherardini (gair-uh-DEE-nee). Gherardini was the wife of a wealthy merchant in Florence.

In da Vinci's time, people had never seen a painting so full of life. Da Vinci painted the subject in a **three-quarter pose**. Her legs were turned to the side, while her torso and face were turned forward. Until then, portraits had been **profiles**. A profile is the outline of someone's face from the side. By turning the person to the front, da Vinci allowed the subject to connect with viewers in a new way.

the *Mona Lisa*

After seeing the *Mona Lisa*, other artists tried to copy da Vinci's techniques. He had made his subject come to life by blurring the lines at the corners of her mouth and eyes. This is called ***sfumato*** (sfoo-MAH-toh). Da Vinci also used a dramatic contrast between light and dark tones, called ***chiaroscuro*** (kee-ahr-uh-SKYOOR-oh).

Da Vinci claimed the *Mona Lisa* had never been completed. He carried it with him for the rest of his life and continued to work on it.

## Mona Lisa's Smile

Mona Lisa is known for her smile. Da Vinci called the work *La Gioconda* (lah jee-oh-KHAN-duh) or *La Joconde* (lah joh-KON-duh). In Italian, this means "joyous" or "happy." The title and the sly smile are believed to be plays on the subject's name. Lisa's married name was *Giocondo*.

## Lasting Beauty

The *Mona Lisa* hangs in its own gallery at the Louvre (LOO-vruh) Museum in Paris, France. It is protected by bullet-proof glass. A special climate-control system keeps the air at 65 degrees Fahrenheit (18 degrees Celsius) with 50 percent humidity. Some have estimated the painting's value at more than $700 million.

People crowd around to see the *Mona Lisa*.

the Louvre Museum in Paris, France

# The Greatest Thinker

In the early 1500s, power was changing hands quickly across Italy. Despite the political changes, Leonardo da Vinci held onto his fame. Rulers wanted this genius in their courts.

For the last years of his life, da Vinci moved from the home of one powerful friend to another. These friends treated him as an honored guest. They gave him comfortable lodging and paid his salary. They asked for little in return.

In 1516, the King of France, François I (fran-SWAH), invited da Vinci to serve as his "First Painter, Architect, and Mechanic." Da Vinci moved to a cozy house in Cloux (kloo), France. He began organizing his notes. He also started designing a palace for the king.

The king visited da Vinci often. He admired da Vinci's mind and liked to hear his ideas. Some say his frequent visits kept da Vinci from completing his last two projects. Both were unfinished when da Vinci died on May 2, 1519. He was 67.

More than 500 years after his death, da Vinci is known as perhaps the greatest thinker of all time. His curiosity was without bounds. His ideas were fresh. And his talent was immeasurable. Da Vinci embodied the spirit of the Renaissance.

self-portrait of
Leonardo da Vinci

## Kind and Gentle

Not only was da Vinci famous for being a genius, but he was also famous for being a nice person. He was gentle and kind, especially to animals. He often bought caged birds at the market just to set them free. He was also a vegetarian, which was rare during that time. According to his journal, he refused to let his body be a tomb for other animals.

## Lost Grave

Da Vinci was buried at the church of Saint Florentin in Amboise (ahm-BWAHZ), France. In 1802, the church and cemetery were destroyed. Today, no one knows the exact location of da Vinci's burial place.

This is the Chateau de Cloux, where da Vinci lived for the last three years of his life.

# Glossary

**altarpieces**—religious paintings that decorate the altars of churches

**apprentice**—a person being trained by a skilled professional to do a trade

**chiaroscuro**—a painting technique using the dramatic contrast between light and dark tones

**city-states**—self-governing states consisting of a city and surrounding territory

**crossbow**—a weapon that fires short, heavy arrows

**dissected**—to have cut apart a formerly living thing to study it

**engineer**—someone who designs, plans, constructs, and maintains things like buildings and machines

**fresco**—the technique of painting on wet plaster

**guilds**—groups of merchants or craftspeople who set trade standards

**illegitimate**—a negative word for a child of unmarried parents

**lyre**—a stringed instrument

**masterpiece**—an exceptional piece of creative work; sometimes refers to the artist's best work

**merchants**—people who buy and sell goods for profit

**notaries**—public officers who witness the making of documents and sign them to show that they are real

**patrons**—people who hire artists to create works of art

**perspective**—adding depth by making objects in the front larger than objects in the back

**profiles**—outlines of people from the side

**realism**—the lifelike representation of people and nature

**renaissance**—French word meaning rebirth; a period of time in which European culture experienced a revival of art, science, and literature

**scientific inquiry**—the method of investigating a subject by first asking questions, then making observations, and finally drawing conclusions

**sfumato**—a painting technique invented by Leonardo da Vinci in which sharp lines are blurred

**three-quarter pose**—a pose in which a subject's knees face to the side while the torso and head face toward the front

**trade**—a job that requires special training or skills

# Index

# Your Turn!

Leonardo da Vinci was an inventor whose ideas were centuries ahead of their time. One of these ideas was a military tank, or armored car. Da Vinci designed a round platform on wheels. The platform was covered by a wooden shell. Eight men rode inside the shell and turned the wheels with a crank.

## Sell that Tank!

Imagine you are a copywriter for a Renaissance advertising agency. You have been assigned to the da Vinci account. Your job is to come up with a clever name for da Vinci's tank. Then, design a brochure to advertise the tanks to rulers of the Italian city-states.